Praise for Storyshares

"One of the brightest innovators and game-changers in the education industry." — Forbes

"Your success in applying research-validated practices to promote literacy serves as a valu-
able model for other organizations seeking to create evidence-based literacy programs."
— Library of Congress

"We need powerful social and educational innovation, and Storyshares is breaking new
ground. The organization addresses critical problems facing our students and teachers. I
am excited about the strategies it brings to the collective work of making sure every
student has an equal chance in life." — Teach For America

"It's the perfect idea. There's really nothing like this. I mean, wow, this will be a wonderful
experience for young people." — Andrea Davis Pinkney, Executive Director, Scholastic

"Reading for meaning opens opportunities for a lifetime of learning. Providing emerging
readers with engaging texts that are designed to offer both challenges and support for each
individual will improve their lives for years to come. Storyshares is a wonderful start."
— David Rose, Co-founder of CAST & UDL

Temperance

Published by Storyshares, LLC
Inspiring reading with a new kind of book.

The characters and events in this book are fictitious. Any similarity to real persons, living or dead, is entirely coincidental.

Storyshares
Storyshares, LLC
24 N. Bryn Mawr Avenue #340
Bryn Mawr, Pennsylvania 19010-3304
www.storyshares.org

Interest Level: Post High School
Grade Level Equivalent: 3.3

ISBN 9798885976244
Book design by Saskia Globig

Author's Note

The goal was always to have my words out there and available to the world. In this moment, you have opened something magical, authentic, and raw. A small portion of my heart, it lays here in your hands. These poems will create questions and pain just as much as clarity and joy. Safe travels as you enter my world that will be mythical and mesmerizing.

Storyshares presents

Temperance

Destany Starr Rodriguez

StoryShares

Thank You for Being Here

Allow yourself to be immersed here.
Where love meets depression,
And drugs meet friendship.
Here you will experience everything,
With just a few words of mine.
You will find stories of what is, and could've been.
Explore bits and pieces of the mind.
The complexities and enchantment of life.
Become infatuated with the torment that is not your own.
And let my sorrow dance on your heart strings.

My Brother Died Years Ago

His heart is still beating today,
Through the hands of God.
The lord nurturing his soul,
Sending him dreams to reach for.
Yet my brother turned his cheek,
Blindly rolling the dice,
Evading snake eyes each time.
Luck is all he has until he doesn't.
Until the lord decides his heart is too heavy to carry.
The very first day he shook the devil's hand,
He surrendered to him.
wo longer qas his head in the clouds,
He has led to quicksand.
paybe the devil keeps him alive,
Forcing him to suffer.
Coercing him to melt into his desires.

Opioids for Dessert

Maybe before bed tonight,
She'll splurge on a few pills.
But just a little taste.
Enough to feel something
But never her own guilt.

Sometimes needles feel better, she says.
Clears her mind faster,
Taking her over the edge
When the pills don't work.
She'll have the sweetest dreams.

She finally dozes off.
From her sweet snacks,
In complete bliss.
She doesn't worry about waking up.

I get to see her shades of purple,
Like blueberry pie.

¡Lavando mis Panties en la ducha!

Skin, raisin and raw,
But I still have to clean myself up.
My brittle fingertips grab hold of the Dove.
A soft aroma finds me for a moment,
distracting me from the memories of that night.
The steam blurs the edges of the panties.

Beginning to lather it between my palms,
Bubbles escaping between the crevices of my fingers.
For a second I think,
Is it normal to be envious of soap?
The soap becomes the harshness of that night.
My grip tightens and I end up kneading them.

I think back to my mother,
And how she taught me how to do this.
How to wash my panties in the shower.

I turn the water cold,
rinsing away all the soap.
And any shame that follows.
I remember to breathe and loosen my grip.
That there is only so much I can do.

My mother would tell me,
Before it goes in the washer,
always rinse in the shower first.

In this case she would tell me,
Before I think about blaming myself,
I have to forgive myself first.

Suicide Letters to Heaven at Ten

God,
If it is you I call upon.
The universe, the stars, or the moon.
Do you hear my calls?
Have you seen my letters?

I've been begging for mercy.
Free me, lord.
I'm shackled in shame.
Burdened by my own existence.

You know the paradox of my life.
Release me.

Now I lay me down to sleep,
I pray the lord my soul to keep...

My Unconscious Mind

I saw my reflection in a dream.

She sat at a creamy white vanity,
The world around her was ethereal.
Pieces of the sun dissolved in the air
and reappeared as her favorite crystals.
The breeze was crisp and somehow she felt warm.
A silent world filled the air,
Pure nothingness,
A realm that was paradisiacal.

A smile stole her face,
And glowed a ray of sunshine.
Her words could cure any second thought.
Her eyes soothed an anxious body.
The touch of her skin was warm,
Inviting anyone to be healed in her arms.
She was made of fire quartz,
Strong and purifying all evil.
She wishes this feeling could last eternally.

But the longer she stared,
that feeling of suffering bloomed.

Rooted in her chest was a rotten heart.
Veins grew in shades of black and crackled like fire.
Eyes welled with acid tears that could never fall,
and a paralyzed face where a smile couldn't exist.
Reality at the forefront,
She had to face it.
Staring into the darkest parts of herself.

I watched myself live her worst nightmare.

Existing in Another World

Beyond what the human eye sees,
There lives a vast pull between my spirit & body.
This realm holds nostalgic scents,
And my most desired sweets.
Melodies that make my body sway,
And hair bounce.
Cotton candy skies that leave me wide eyed.
And an ocean that olers me grace.

In the wind I hear my dad's laugh,
And feel my mom's touch.
Stunned by the breeze,
I'm awakened from my fantasy.

I am pulled back to earth.
Where pretending is difficult.
The real world, where everything hurts.
A wound with salt,
And tears that burn.

Hell on Earth

My nights are sleepless, but I still wake up.
I put my hand on the stove, but it was off.
I pifk up the pen to write stories,
but your name ends up in fine print.
I won the marathon, but I was barefoot.
My wine tastes good, but better in a broken glass.
I kiss your lips, but you bite your tongue.

Are you my punishment?
The inside of my body itches.

mOoD sWiNgS

When the rest of the world goes dark,
And in my bed alone I lie.
Where thoughts become demons,
And my own skin burns of hatred.
Grasping onto this idea of life,
And if the hurt is worth more days here.

But just like that I am okay.
Mind is as clear as the sky in August,
A free bird feeling the warm breeze.
Within me is a calm heart,
enveloped with tranquility.

Yet my internal monologue speaks miserably.
A silver tongue of evil.
In a blink of an eye, I am critical,
Too aware of myself,
And the way I am perceived.
I reek of rage and sorrow.

All in the matter of minutes.

A Prayer for God's Favor

And if I could only pray once more in this life,
I'd rest my knees on the cherry wood floor.
Let my shoulder glades kiss gently,
while my palms cradle one another.
Give my heart & breath a moment to coalesce.
Grant my mind a moment of equanimity.

I'd thank the Universe for her patience,
Pay homage to all she has sacrifced for me.
Commend her assiduous labor,
and celebrate her victories.

The Universe would show gratitude.
For my kind words, a favor.
She'd ask how she could aid me.
To which I'd respond,
free my soul from my body.

I Love You, I Love You, I Love You

You've become my bittersweet oasis.
A place I wanna stay and linger in forever.
Your touch is just like sand, with words as warm as the sun.
Chinola lips, coconut rind eyes, a rhythmic heartbeat.

You feel just like home.

A Witches' Den

It's warm here.
Makes you catch your breath.
You don't mind though.
With every step you take,
You become more mesmerized.
This is like nothing you've ever seen before.

Inside this den there is more.
There is passion, lust, and love.
A feeling so infnite.
Deep in the underground.
A rich, earthly place to call home.
You never want to leave.

Here in my sanctuary.
Only you are invited.
You get one chance.
If you last in my oasis,
then forever mine, you be.

Achilles Heel

With the gift within me,
I can do anything.
I am powerful. I am immense.
My abilities go beyond the five senses.
If I want it, I will have it.

But I found my kryptonite.

A sensation of the heart.
A feeling that consumes the body.
Makes you do things you'd never do.
Say things unimaginable.
This is where my heel sinks.

Don't Burn Me Out, but Let Me Go

You lit your candle and refused to release me.
Let the kicper of the kame rewresent our story now,
A slow burn.
The charcoaled wax popping into the air,
making its way back down to the melted lava of mahogany.

Allow me to blend into another lost memory.
Flames and passion intertwine like our lips on nights of love.
Our souls fearful of one another's evanescence.
Nostalgia for this feeling will free you in another life.

I've been burning for a lifetime with you.
But my wick is burnt out.
So do me a favor and submerge me.
Grant yourself the freedom,
Drown me in your favorite stories of us.
Orom the first night with a Virvo moon,
to last night's Aries.

Forget me not, mi cielo.
Just allow someone else to light my candle.

The Father, the Son, and the Holy Spirit

In my father's hands I lay,
Where calluses form and create a thick coven,
of what should be my safe haven.
Yet in these palms I feel the draft between the crevices.
The roughness scratching my skin.
I become raw.
I'm ripped and shredded,
By the man who is supposed to love and forgive all.
I'm tortured by the chambers his commandments create.

The blood of his son burns my body whole,
Inside out.
Leaving me with nothing but a dying heart.
He sacrifces it for another version of me
In a different life.
He says I'll learn my lesson then.

The spirit takes me,
Down a body of water where I shall be reborn.
I'll enter the world forgetting all I know of religion.
He hopes I'll find him again,
And repent for my past self.

I DON'T FEEL THIS ANYMORE

I always knew.
One way or another.
You'd be mine,
And I'd be yours.

Then we kissed.
Then we cried.

Maybe not right now,
But you'll be mine again soon.

And I'll be yours.

Bah-Humbug

Wrapped around a humbug's finger,
This love had been so intoxicating.
A witch and his cauldron,
Overflowing with diabolical mixture.
In a dark room filled with mist alongside sudden flashes,
Sparks collided in the air.
I couldn't look away.
The aroma swept me off the ground.
I was under his spell.
With his silver tongue and crystal ball,
He told me everything I needed to hear.
He told me that we were what he had been waiting for.
I should've looked more closely at his crystal ball.
It was made of stone.
Crevices were filled with his brew.
He knew what he was doing when I looked into his eyes.
He burned me,
And turned my heart to stone.
Bah-Humbug.

The Backfire of Russian Roulette

There are no words for this.
I've surpassed my tipping point time and time again.
Drenched in shame,
Consumed in your shallowness.
This is beyond embarrassment,
My ego has been crushed.

You knew better, but you did it anyway.
Yet there I stood,
Confidently in your shadow.
Admiring you blindly.
Convinced that love and pain were parallel.

Truth be told my beloved,
I am enraged.
Leel my wrath as your shadow grows small.

Let loneliness devour you.
Allow every teardrop to come,
And burn like streams of acid.

When your heart aches with the disappearance of me,
Accept the agony of your decisions.
Your own emotions will consume your being.

When you beg for mercy,
I will withhold sympathy.
For I will not stop the bleeding,
Of the wound you self-inflicted.

Where a Chance Would Have Led Us

We were untouched,
by any and all lingering thoughts of the world.
It had been you and me.
Our little safe haven.
The sweet nothings & exchange of art.

This wasn't because of fate,
you spoke your words with intention.
Every breath was purposeful.

I think I could've learned to love you.
If you hadn't gone so soon.

Ghosts Aren't Scary After All

Does it feel a bit odd to you?
To be accustomed to one's energy and long for it.
But just as quickly as you want it,
you want nothing to do with it too.
Do your days weigh a bit more?
When the burden of your choice faces you at trial,
and you have to dig out your own grave?
Have sudden flashes disrupted your day?
A voice humming in your ear.

The absence of each other is odd.
But endures, nonetheless.
Two souls meant to meet,
and perhaps to never meet again.

What a Feeling

Engulfed in his fiery desire for love,
Tangled in his passionate ways,
We lay side by side with our limbs intertwined.
This arrangement felt eternal.
Stories, kisses, and dreams exchanged between intimacy.
Giggling like school children.
We dined, sipped and became elevated.
I stared confidently into his eyes,
Never became lost in them, I felt this was my path.
Traced my fingertips on every inch of his body,
I could find him with my eyes closed.
My soul experienced euphoria as it laced with his aura.
A safety net of love, lust, and security.

Was this a fever dream?

Strawberry Margarita With A Sugar Rim

They used to ask me what I like to drink.
I'd say something sweet but strong.
I didn't like to taste the liquor,
but I loved the feeling.

When I'd take a sip,
I wanted it to feel like nothing before.

When my veins were fueled with Tequila,
Pulsing a Merengue rhythm,
The blood would rush to my cheeks,
And everyone would know I was having a good time.

When the drink started to taste like juice,
I'd begin slowly sliding my tongue on the rim.
Salt was too bitter and familiar,
Felt like hands in places they shouldn't be.

No longer will I let salt scar my tongue.
I want something sweet.
Something so memorable.

But this time when I sit at the bar,
And they ask me what I want to drink,
I say, "water."

I NEED TO FIND MY WAY HOME

Our taino line is a mystery befriended by pain.
We became accustomed to secrecy,
while drowning in the Caribbean sea.
Salt burns our eyes and nose,
but heals our skin and heart.
Choking on centuries of trauma,
Yet somehow we can still swim.

I sink into the vast ocean every time.
I cry, and I cry, and I cry.
My tears hold the stories I am afraid to tell.
Praying for my ancestors to lead me.
To release the burdens gripping my spirit and body.

Maybe they'll hear my heartbeat mimic the bayohabao.
Maybe their spirits will rise,
and all the devastation will go away.

Maybe this bloodline can make suffering feel beautiful.

I Wish I Could Tell You This,
but I'll Write It Instead

I am still trying to learn how to love you.

To love you despite your absence.
To love you through your trauma.
To love you knowing there are decades of lies.
To love you with your lack of touch.
To love you, even though you don't know who I am.

How can I love a stranger that I've known my whole life?

Because I love you though you left.
Because I love you though I know nothing of you.
Because I love you when you withhold the truth.
Because I love you when you try to hold me.
Because I love you for pretending to know me.

I've always known how to love you.

Lydia and Ramona.
My Great Grandmother and Mama.

For their hands were so gentle, and their voices so kind.
And although language halted our communication,
their love radiated through affection.
There was never a moment of doubt that you both were my
     angels on earth.

With your cosmic travels, I pray for your eternal peace.
As you guide me through this life, and the next.

I love you infinitely.

Cosmic Travels

Glitter limbs outstretched in ways never seen before.
Shrunken at the root.
Resembles nothingness.
You lose human form
becoming something great.
Shimmers of light and love.
Glistening reflections of purity.
Everything someone wants to see.
Loss of physical becomes an aura.
Hues of blue,
The putter of a jay,
Expansive seas,
As immense as the sky.

Flourishing in the stars,
Kissed by the moon,
Hugged in the warmth of the sun.
From our world to the next realm.
You're ready.
Your travels are beautiful.
Your confirmation is not a rainy day,
Not a rainbow in the sky.
Not a moment near the ocean,
Or clearest of skies.

It lays on my chest, your testimony.
Consuming my entirety,
I experience peace for the first time since your
　　　　cosmic travel.

Island of Enchantment

As the soles of my feet join the sand,
The sand that holds all the stories of my ancestors,
I find myself shut eye and floating.
Although darkness falls,
The warmth of the sun pulls me into an embrace.
Maracas in the distance create a soft melody,
Gentle rattles raise the hairs along my skin.
Drums make way,
And reflect my heart's rhythm.
Allowing me to fully emerge,
in the sweet whispers of my antecedents.
Losing my soul in the best way possible.
On the island of enchantment.

Ethereal Being

I stretch out my arms and elongate my fingers
Admiring the slow movement
Palms facing outwards
Feeling the gentle stretch on my wrist.

Am I satisfied with what I see in front of me?
I pull myself to the mirror
It reflects the hues of my aura
I am green, white, and pink
Grounded, Aligned, and Receptive.

Placing my body flat on the cold wooden floor,
Waiting for my body to mold.
Meld into the ground beneath.
Closing my eyes, relaxing my shoulders, and breathing
1, 2, 3
Slowly, heaviness consumes me.
4, 5, 6
From the heels of my feet,
And earthly thighs.
My back reminiscent of the ocean.
It is Strong.
7, 8, 9
I know where I am.
10.

I've ascended to a place where no one has gone before
I am not floating, walking, standing or running.
I am existing.
I am existing where there is no sky,
And no ground.

I am existing where there is no man, or woman.
I am existing where there is no life
There is no god.
Yet this time,
When my palms run ahead of me,

They glow.
A radiant beam no one has seen before
And with every movement I make
Glowing light drips off my being
These drips take me to the abyss above.
Disintegrating.
It is not painful,
I only feel peace.

Breathing.
10
My heart is calm.
9
My eyes begin to open.
8
The tip of my nose,
7
and fingers,
6
and toes slightly chilled

5
My mind capturing serenity
4
I realize something
3
I am not bones, and flesh.
2
I am simply stardust.
1.

Acknowledgments

There are quite a few people I'd like to thank, but especially Louise Baigelman, Angela Dellisola, and Meredith Mix. These three incredible women have been supporting me from the very beginning, and were a part of every step throughout this process. They believed in me, my words, and everything in between. To Kerri Brown McCarron, for showing me as a young adult that writing and poetry were my passion. Josh DoBell for reigniting the fire underneath my feet when it comes to writing freely, and from your heart. Finally, to my parents: your unconditional love throughout life has allowed me to be the person I have always wanted to be — a writer.

About the Author

Destany Starr Rodriguez is a contributing author to the Storyshares library.

About the Publisher

Storyshares is a publisher focused on supporting the millions of teens and adults who struggle with reading by creating a new shelf in the library specifically for them. The ever-growing collection features content that is compelling and culturally relevant for teens and adults, yet still readable at a range of lower reading levels.

Storyshares generates content by engaging deeply with writers, bringing together a community to create this new kind of book. With more intriguing and approachable stories to choose from, the teens and adults who have fallen behind are improving their skills and beginning to discover the joy of reading. For more information, visit storyshares.org.

Easy to read. Hard to put down.

Milton Keynes UK
Ingram Content Group UK Ltd.
UKHW020952221123
433051UK00021B/1304